D1120168

TA-POO-ACH MEANS APPLE

Written and Illustrated by

BARBARA GENET

Alternatives in Religious Education, Inc.
Denver, Colorado

Published by Alternatives in Religious Education, Inc.
3945 South Oneida Street, Denver, Colorado 80237

Library of Congress Cataloging in Publication Data

Genet, Barbara, 1933–
Ta-poo-ach means apple.

Tapuaḥ on dust jacket.
Summary: Captioned illustrations introduce the letters
of the Hebrew alphabet and common Hebrew words,
from ta-poo-ach (apple) to ra-keh-vet (train)
1. Hebrew language — Alphabet — Juvenile literature.
[1. Hebrew language — Alphabet.   2. Alphabet]
I. Title.   II. Title: Tapuaḥ.
PJ4589.G53   492.4'81 [E]   85–60009

ISBN: 0-86705-015-2

Printed in the United States of America
First Edition
10   9   8   7   6   5   4   3   2   1

Dedicated to

AMY SAUL ELLEN LANE JACKIE STEVE MOTHER

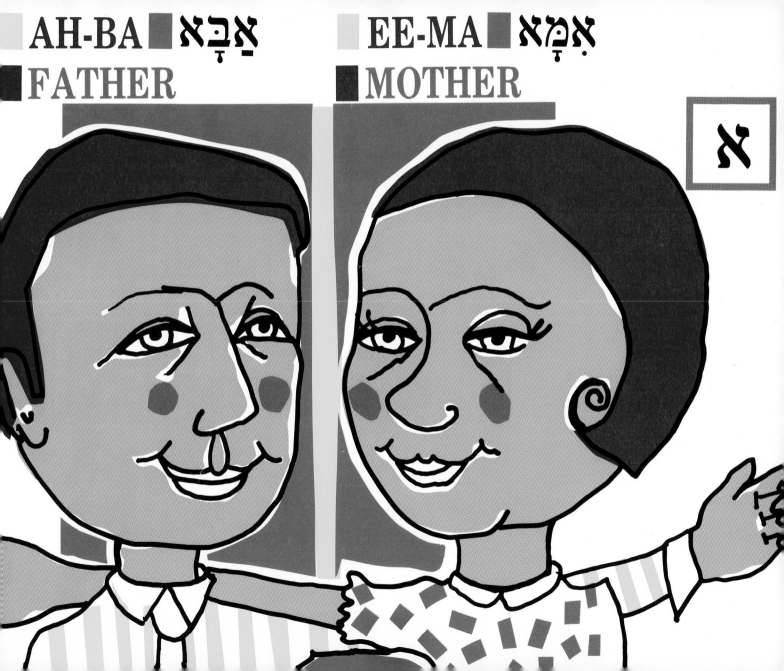

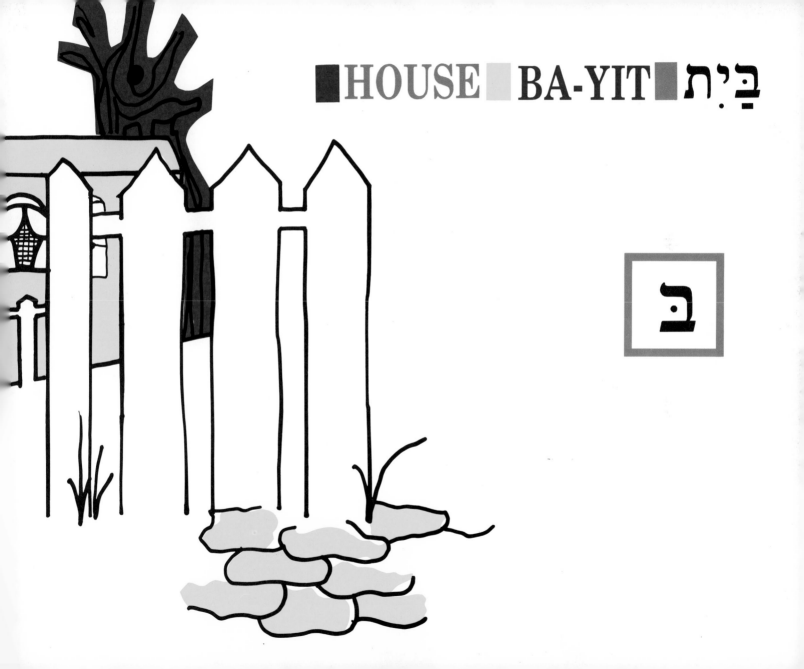

HOUSE BA-YIT בַּיִת

ב

גְּלִידָה

G'LEE-DAH

ICE CREAM

הֶגֶה

HEH-GEH

STEERING WHEEL

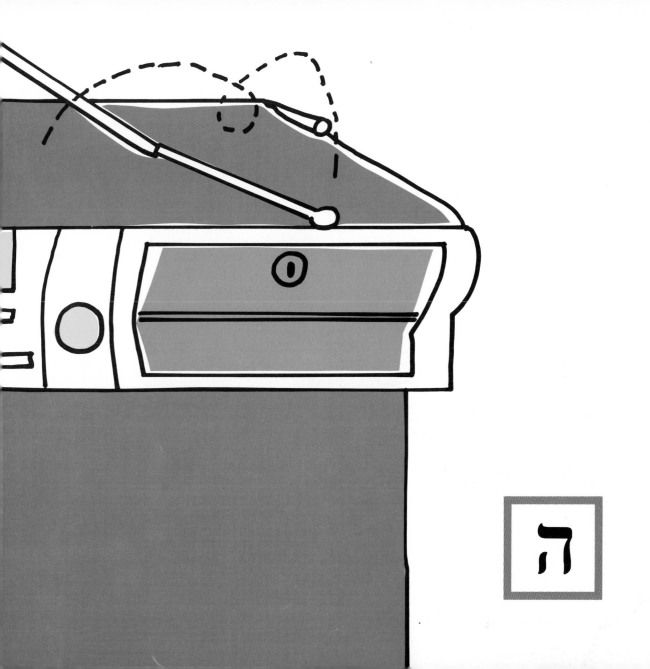

ה

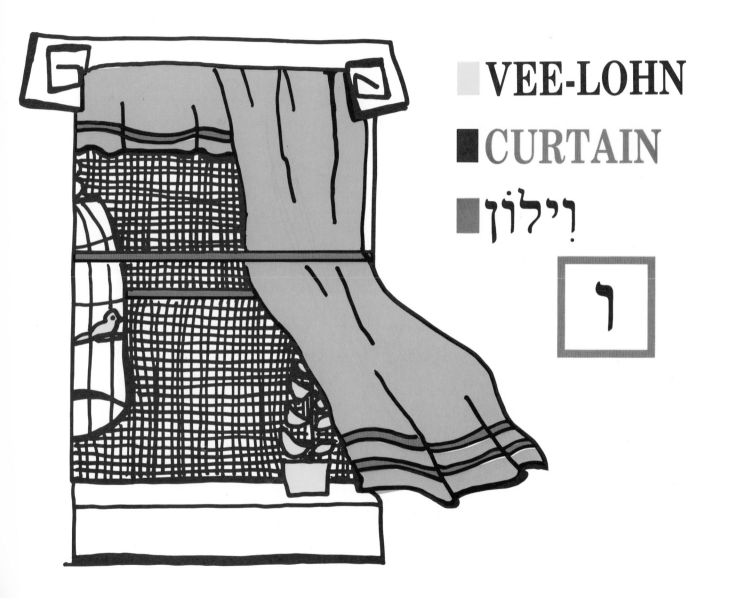

VEE-LOHN

CURTAIN

וִילוֹן

ו

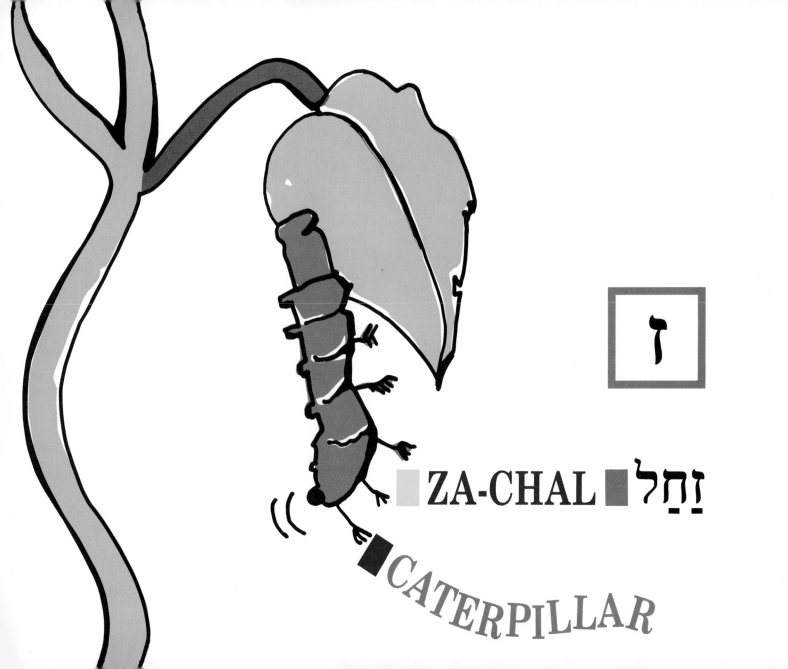

ז

ZA-CHAL זַחַל

CATERPILLAR

חֲצוֹצְרָה

CHA-TZOTZ-RAH

TRUMPET

ח

TELEPHONE ■ TE-LE-FOHN ■ טֶלֶפוֹן

owry St--------------245-8418   Towbin Saul 1520 NE 11th St-----------247-0090   Towbin Mike 220 NE 12th Av------246-2976
den & Supplies   Towbin Richard 3583 SW 14th Av---------245-2753   Towbin Marty 17 NW 2nd Av-------247-8467   Tri-State Dusting
    15335 SW 288th St 247-3660   Towbin Beth 26627 SW 8th St------------246-2951   Towbin Mitchell 34945 SW 18-----228-9111   Tri-Time Inc 800 12
SW 144th Av----------248-3948   Towbin Karen 2245 SW 23rd St-----------241-2235   Towbin Peter 2247 S Oklahoma Av 247-0990   Triana Robert 1522 SW
80 SW 214th Jackson--247-6183   Towbin Samuel 2595 E 63rd Way----------244-9078   Towbin Robert 2245 W 15th St----258-1813   Triana Samuel 7653 E
  1212 NW 9th Av Ctr--315-6692   Towbin Stuart 955 W 14th Ave-----------369-1157   Towbin Ronald 38152 E. 105th----331-1616   Tribble Sam 7712 W Gay

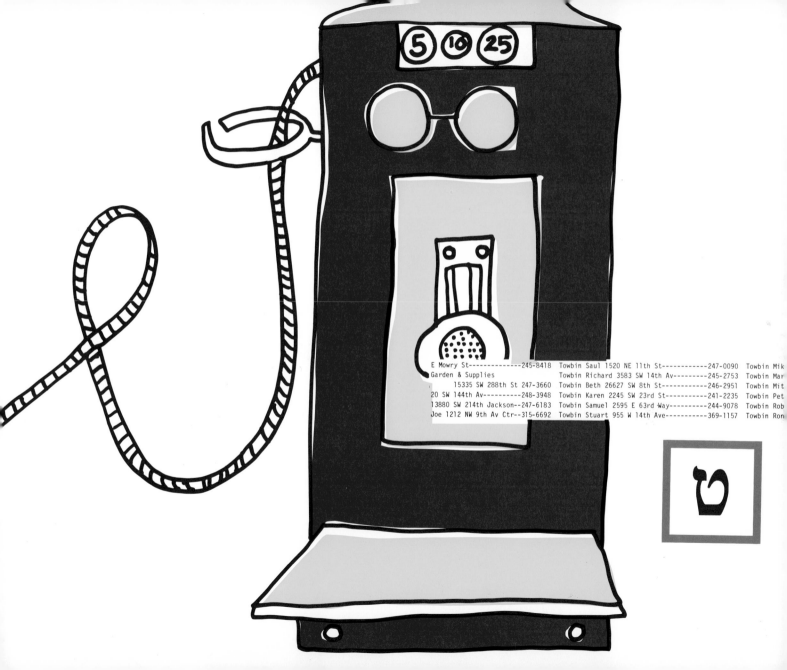

E Mowry St--------------245-8418   Towbin Saul 1520 NE 11th St-----------247-0090   Towbin Mik
Garden & Supplies   Towbin Richard 3583 SW 14th Av---------245-2753   Towbin Mar
        15335 SW 288th St 247-3660 Towbin Beth 26627 SW 8th St------------246-2951   Towbin Mit
20 SW 144th Av----------248-3948   Towbin Karen 2245 SW 23rd St-----------241-2235   Towbin Pet
13880 SW 214th Jackson--247-6183   Towbin Samuel 2595 E 63rd Way----------244-9078   Towbin Rob
Joe 1212 NW 9th Av Ctr--315-6692   Towbin Stuart 955 W 14th Ave-----------369-1157   Towbin Ron

יְלָדִים

Y'LA-DEEM

CHILDREN

י

TEMPLE BETH AM

 K'TAY-FOHT ■ כְּתֵפוֹת

■ SUSPENDERS

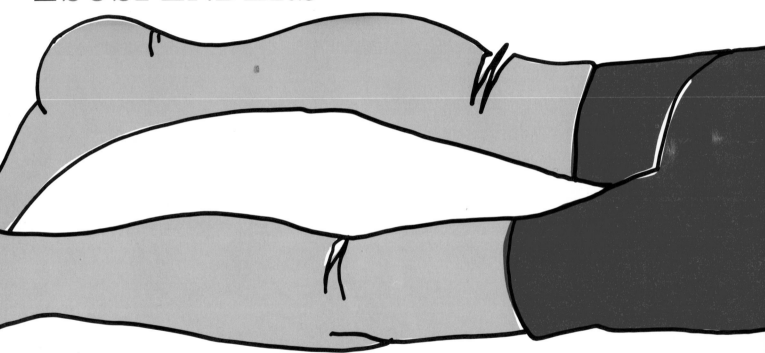

■ BUTTON ■ KAF-TOR ■ כַּפְתּוֹר

KEE-PAH כִּפָּה

CAP

 כ

POCKET KEES כִּיס

ל

■CLOWN ■LAY-TZAN ■לֵיצָן

■KEY ■MAF-TAY-ACH■מַפְתֵּחַ

מ

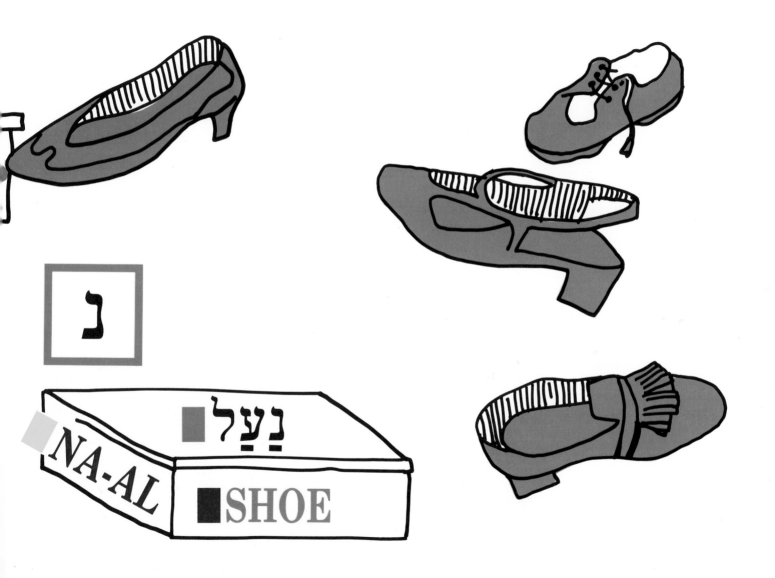

נ

נַעַל

NA-AL ■SHOE

סִירָה

SEE-RAH

BOAT

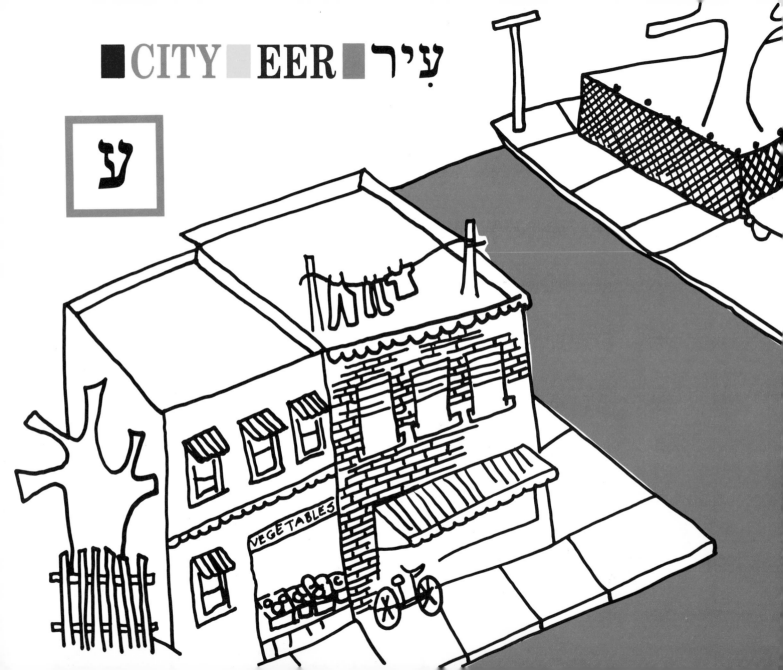

CITY EER עִיר

ע

VEGETABLES

ELEPHANT PEEL פִּיל

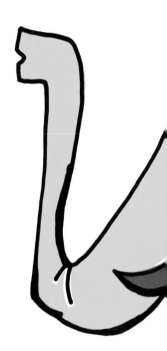

■BIRD ■TSEE-POR■ צִפּוֹר

צ

MONKEY **KOHF** קוף

ק

TRAIN ■ RA-KEH-VET ■ רַכֶּבֶת

ר

CLOCK **SHA-OHN** שָׁעוֹן

LIPS S'FA-TA-YIM שְׂפָתַיִם

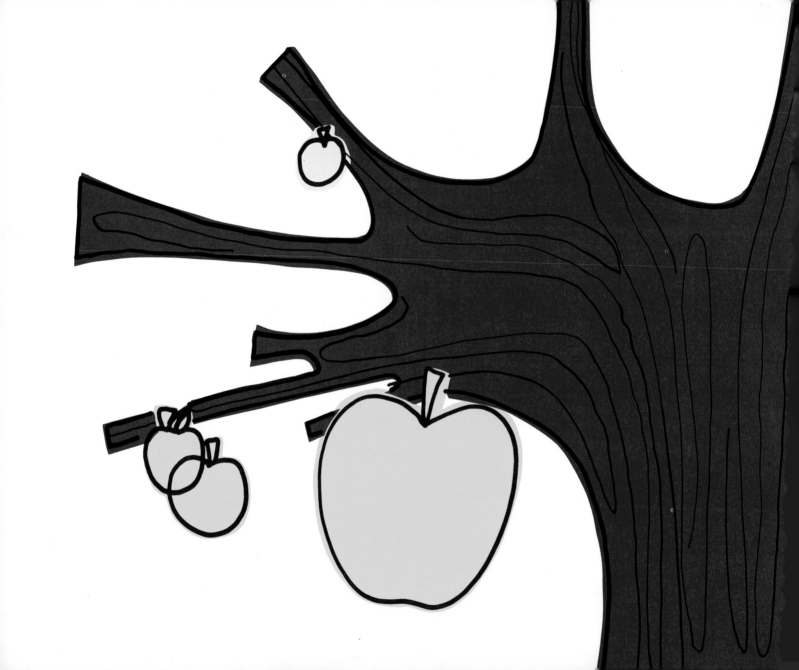

APPLE TA-POO-ACH תַּפּוּחַ

תּ